everyday **STEM**

ENGINEERING

CIVIL ENGINEERING

Engineering is all around you

KINGFISHER
LONDON & NEW YORK

First published 2022 in the United States by Kingfisher
120 Broadway, New York, NY 10271
Kingfisher is an imprint of Macmillan Children's Books, London
All rights reserved.

Copyright © Macmillan Publishers
International Ltd 2022

ISBN 978-0-7534-7823-3

Distributed in the U.S. and Canada by Macmillan,
120 Broadway, New York, NY 10271

Library of Congress Cataloging-in-Publication data has been applied for.

Author: Jenny Jacoby
Illustrator: Luna Valentine
Series editor: Lizzie Davey
Series design: Jim Green

Kingfisher Books are available for special promotions and premiums.
For details contact:
Special Markets Department, Macmillan
120 Broadway, New York, NY 10271.

For more information please visit:
www.kingfisherbooks.com

Printed in China
2 4 6 8 9 7 5 3 1
1TR/0722/UG/WKT/128MA

EU representative: 1st Floor, The Liffey Trust Centre
117-126 Sheriff Street Upper, Dublin 1 D01 YC43

CONTENTS

WHAT IS ENGINEERING?

Engineering is inventing tools to solve problems and improve lives. Engineers use their scientific, technological, and mathematical knowledge to figure out how to bring creative ideas for useful inventions to life. They are creative inventors and focused problem solvers. The work engineers do is often divided into two areas: civil and mechanical engineering.

CIVIL ENGINEERING

This type of engineering is about creating the structures you see around you—the roads, buildings, transportation systems, hospitals, power supplies, and many other vital things you use daily without thinking much about. Civil engineering is not always about creating new things but about making sure that existing structures remain safe and efficient— and looking to see how they can be improved.

Engineers think about the best materials to use.

Builders work closely with engineers to make sure the plans are followed.

4

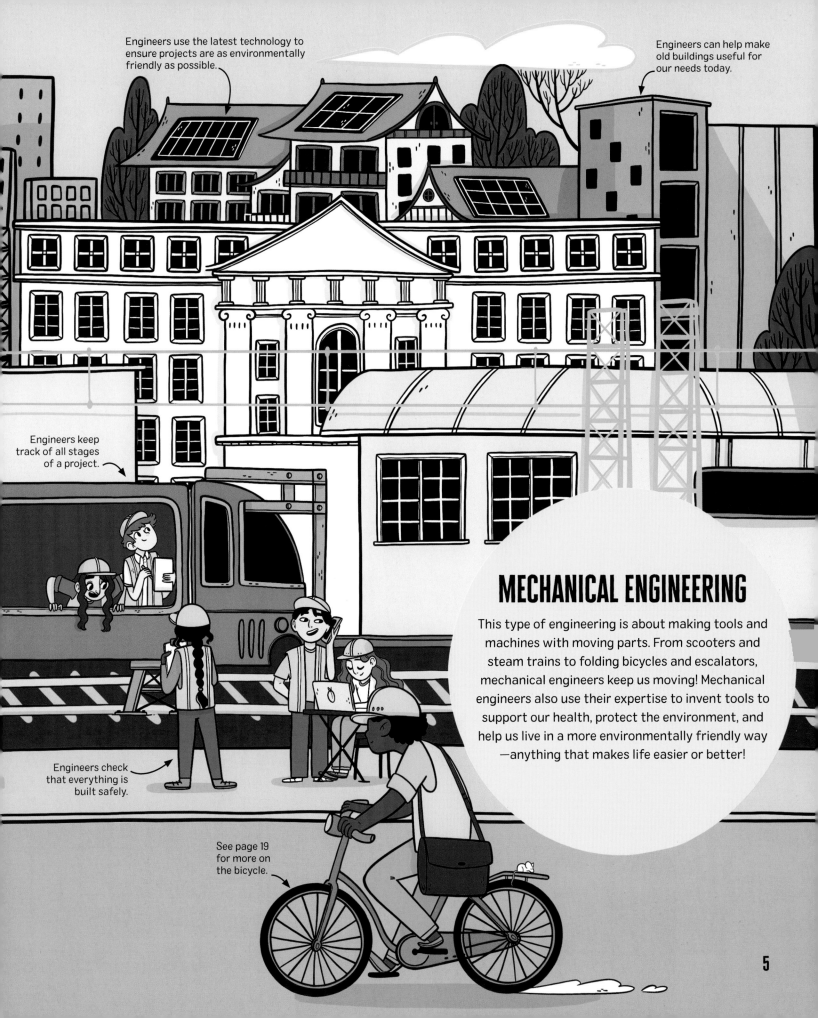

Engineers use the latest technology to ensure projects are as environmentally friendly as possible.

Engineers can help make old buildings useful for our needs today.

Engineers keep track of all stages of a project.

Engineers check that everything is built safely.

See page 19 for more on the bicycle.

MECHANICAL ENGINEERING

This type of engineering is about making tools and machines with moving parts. From scooters and steam trains to folding bicycles and escalators, mechanical engineers keep us moving! Mechanical engineers also use their expertise to invent tools to support our health, protect the environment, and help us live in a more environmentally friendly way —anything that makes life easier or better!

ENGINEERING SKILLS

Engineers need to know a lot about math and science, and because there is so much to know and explore, they study for many years. However, there are many different skills involved in being a great engineer. School helps you learn some of those skills, and there are others you are probably already an expert in!

Math classes teach us how to play with numbers and find patterns. We can discover how to build strong structures by measuring angles and understanding how shapes work together.

Science teaches us how to observe and measure the world and encourages us to have ideas and test them out.

Playing and exploring gives us plenty of chances to **solve problems**. Engineers don't let problems stop their plans—and neither do we when we are playing!

Observing the world is an easy way to find out how things work, and it can inspire brand new ideas.

In **design** classes we learn to test out our creativity, which helps us solve problems.

TEAMWORK

No single engineer is the best at all of these skills. This is why it's important to work as a team, with different people bringing their different skills together. Amazing engineering feats can happen when we work together!

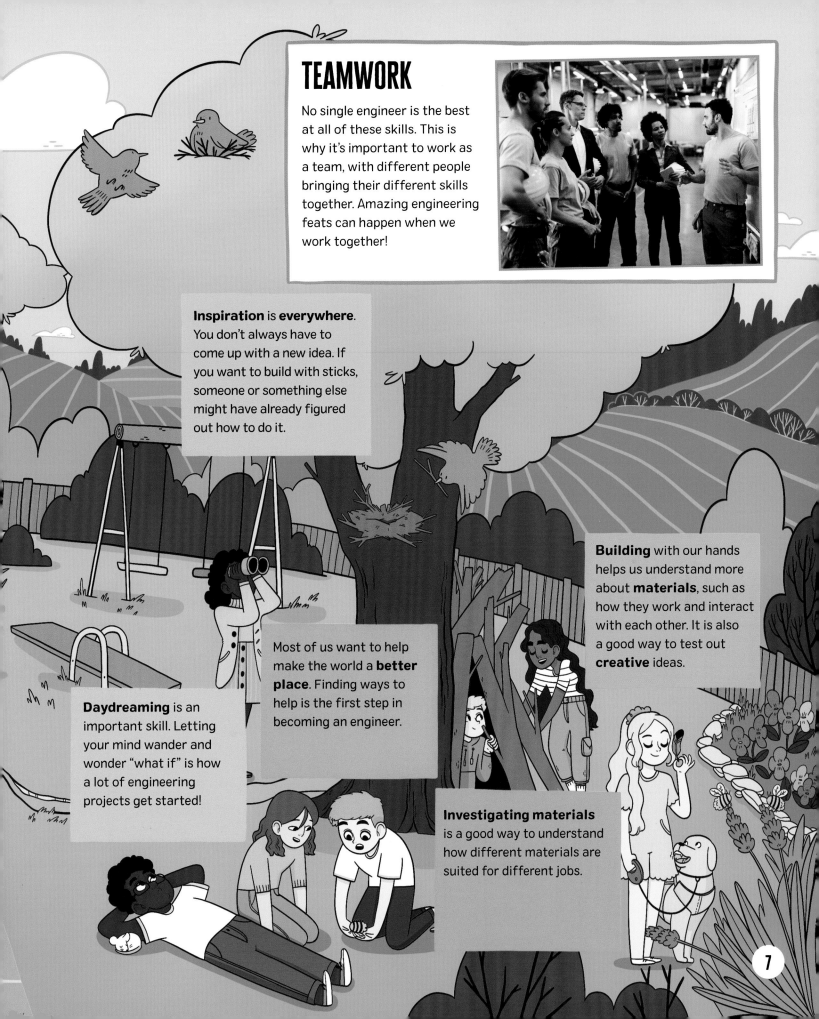

Inspiration is **everywhere**. You don't always have to come up with a new idea. If you want to build with sticks, someone or something else might have already figured out how to do it.

Building with our hands helps us understand more about **materials**, such as how they work and interact with each other. It is also a good way to test out **creative** ideas.

Most of us want to help make the world a **better place**. Finding ways to help is the first step in becoming an engineer.

Daydreaming is an important skill. Letting your mind wander and wonder "what if" is how a lot of engineering projects get started!

Investigating materials is a good way to understand how different materials are suited for different jobs.

THE SHARD

Let's take a look at The Shard: an iconic building on the skyline of London, England, right next to the River Thames. The Shard is the tallest tower in western Europe, with 87 stories and 44 elevators. The triangular shape of its design was inspired by the spires of London's churches and the masts of tall ships.

INSIDE THE SHARD

This skyscraper is made from . . .

- **1.9 million cu. ft. (54,000 m³) of concrete**, which would fill 22 Olympic swimming pools.

- **1,000 glass panels**—enough to cover 10 football fields.

- The steel in the building weighs **12,5000 metric tonnes**—more than 70 blue whales!

The spire at the top of The Shard is made from steel painted with special paint to protect it from the wind and Sun.

The core of the building is made from concrete, which is strong enough to resist the wind.

The framework is made from steel beams and columns. Steel was used because it's strong but relatively light.

The paneling is made from extra-white glass, which reflects the colors around it, so that the building appears to change with the seasons.

The foundations extend 175 ft. (54 m) below the ground.

ROMA AGRAWAL (BORN 1983)

Agrawal grew up in Mumbai, London, and New York. She loved to play with toy bricks, building and destroying to find out how things were made.

She studied physics at the University of Oxford and structural engineering at Imperial College London.

Agrawal spent six years working as a structural engineer on The Shard.

Not many women work in the construction industry, and she was often the only woman in meetings. It took time for her to feel confident enough to speak up.

Our future engineers need to be curious, work well with others, think creatively, and make things!

Now Agrawal works to encourage more women and people from diverse backgrounds to start careers in engineering.

ENGINEERING EVERYWHERE

The engineered world is all around us! Engineers have influenced your day even when you're going for a walk out in the wilds of nature—an engineer has designed the vehicle you arrived in, the road or path you traveled on, and maybe even some of your equipment.

Engineers helped design this building, which is currently under construction. They are on site to solve any problems while it's being built.

These solar panels turn the Sun's energy into electricity to provide power to this house.

Traffic lights control the flow of traffic to keep everybody safe. Pedestrians press a button to let the system know when they want to cross the road.

Engineers figured out the best materials to keep the roads strong under a lot of traffic, and they included a slight slope to allow the rain to run off into the gutters.

Pipes carrying important things like electricity, natural gas, and water are kept safe underground. Access points are positioned at regular intervals in case people need to fix any problems.

ENGINEERING THROUGH TIME

Humans have been building structures for many thousands of years. We started off building and engineering for our most important needs: shelter and hunting animals to eat. Much of this early engineering has been lost to history, but there are plenty of amazing ancient structures around the world that are still standing—and that tell a story about what was important to the people who built them.

PONT DU GARD, FRANCE (A.D. 60)

The Romans built this aqueduct to bring fresh water to the 50,000 people who lived in Nîmes, France. Romans were great civil engineers—they built structures like this to support city life wherever they settled.

The Pont du Gard has survived well because its arches are strong and well built. The arches support the weight above by transferring the force downward into the stable stone columns. The rocks were cut very precisely so that each one fits into place without any mortar being needed to hold them together.

CHICHEN ITZA PYRAMID, MEXICO (A.D. 400–500)

The ancient city of Chichen Itza in Mexico was one of the largest Mayan cities. The site is filled with ruins of Mayan buildings, of which the pyramid is the most famous. The pyramid was built as a temple to the god Kukulcan. Reaching the temple at the top takes 91 steps, and there is a staircase on each of the four sides. Along the staircases are sculptures of feathered serpents. On the spring and fall equinoxes, the sunlight makes triangular shadows on one of the pyramid's sides, making it look like the serpent is crawling down the pyramid. The Mayan engineers who built this pyramid built a structure strong enough to last centuries while also designing the building to interact with the natural world.

THE GREAT WALL, CHINA (A.D. 1368–1644)

The Great Wall of China was built by Ming emperors to keep out invaders from Mongolia. The oldest parts of the wall are 2,300 years old. Sections of it were joined together over time, and by 1644 it looked how it does today.

The wall makes the most of natural defenses—mountain ridges, cliffs, and rivers. Its man-made defenses have three main structures:

• The wall, which is thicker at the bottom for strength and stability and around 25 ft. (8 m) tall.

• Passes, which are like small forts and are built at regular intervals. They allow people and goods to pass through the wall using a ramp or ladder.

• Signal towers at the highest points of the wall, where soldiers were stationed. They sent messages along the line using fires and smoke signals.

ROYAL CRESCENT, UK (A.D. 1774)

The elegant sweeping semicircle of this residential street in Bath, England, was designed in the height of Georgian fashion. Architects of the time were fascinated with classical Italy as well as elegance and order. The 500 ft. (150 m) long Royal Crescent has a uniform front, with each home facing the parkland across the street. The front has classical columns at regular intervals along its length, giving a sense of order and elegance. The grandeur of the building's design is one of the reasons it has been so well taken care of over the centuries.

BROOKLYN BRIDGE

The Brooklyn Bridge in New York City was the longest bridge in the world when it opened in 1883. It was the first suspension bridge to use steel wires, with stronger cables than had ever been seen before. To build the bridge's support towers, workers had to dig underwater into the riverbed, deeper than ever before. The Brooklyn Bridge broke engineering records, but this progress came at the cost of many lives, including that of its original architect, John Roebling.

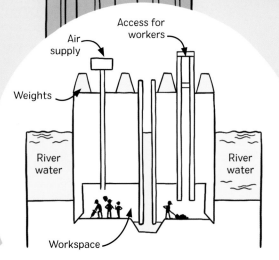

Air supply

Access for workers

Weights

River water

River water

Workspace

BUILDING UNDERWATER

To allow workers to dig and build on the riverbed, engineers use a "caisson." This is an airtight room underwater—like when you put an upside-down cup into a bowl of water, trapping air inside.

The problem with working deep underwater is that the pressure is very strong, which affects the body. If you travel back up to the surface too quickly, it can cause a painful condition called "caisson disease." Because doctors didn't understand about caisson disease at the time, workers got sick, and many died.

ENGINEERING FAMILY

Two days into the construction of his great design, John Roebling had an accident on site and died. His son Washington took over but then became bedridden with caisson disease. Fortunately, Washington's wife, Emily, was educated and interested in engineering, and she took over from Washington. In the 1800s it was unheard-of to have women on construction sites, but Emily was able to use her husband's knowledge and her own management skills to solve design problems. She managed the project for eleven years and was the first to cross the bridge on opening day.

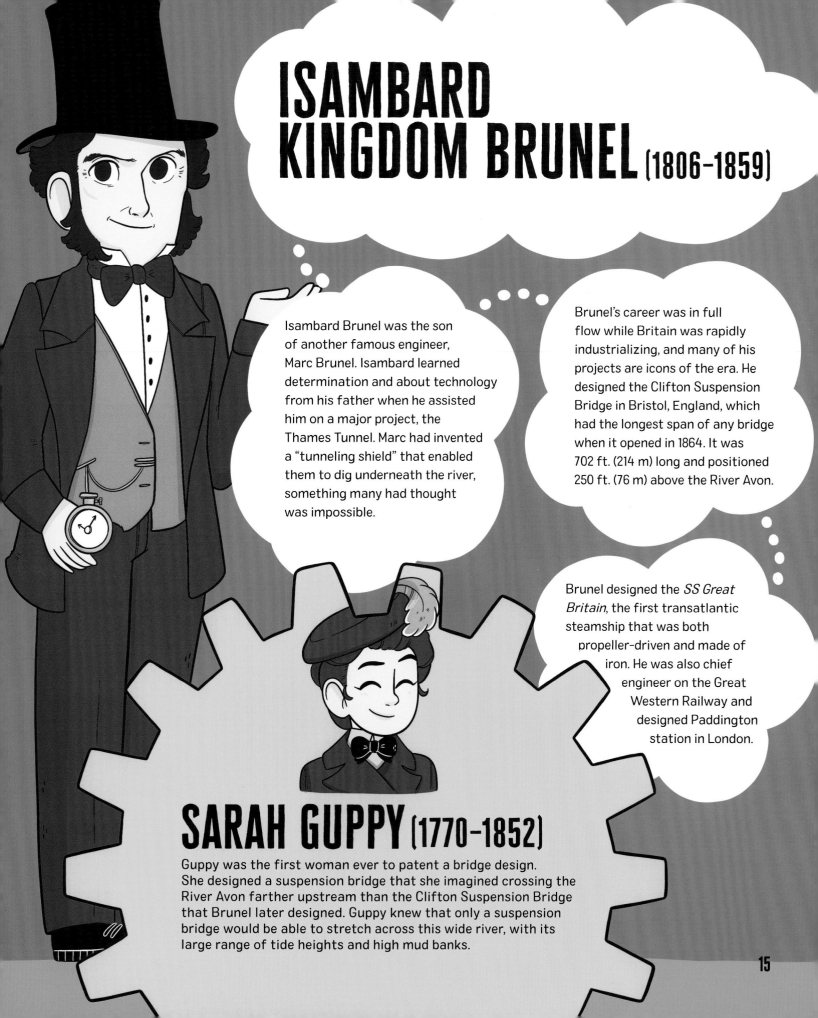

ISAMBARD KINGDOM BRUNEL (1806–1859)

Isambard Brunel was the son of another famous engineer, Marc Brunel. Isambard learned determination and about technology from his father when he assisted him on a major project, the Thames Tunnel. Marc had invented a "tunneling shield" that enabled them to dig underneath the river, something many had thought was impossible.

Brunel's career was in full flow while Britain was rapidly industrializing, and many of his projects are icons of the era. He designed the Clifton Suspension Bridge in Bristol, England, which had the longest span of any bridge when it opened in 1864. It was 702 ft. (214 m) long and positioned 250 ft. (76 m) above the River Avon.

Brunel designed the *SS Great Britain*, the first transatlantic steamship that was both propeller-driven and made of iron. He was also chief engineer on the Great Western Railway and designed Paddington station in London.

SARAH GUPPY (1770–1852)

Guppy was the first woman ever to patent a bridge design. She designed a suspension bridge that she imagined crossing the River Avon farther upstream than the Clifton Suspension Bridge that Brunel later designed. Guppy knew that only a suspension bridge would be able to stretch across this wide river, with its large range of tide heights and high mud banks.

ENGINEERED TOGETHER

Engineering brings people together. It makes it easier to travel quickly and comfortably and visit people and places, and it helps people communicate across large distances. The more we know each other, the more we understand each other and the better we can work together. Here are a few examples of engineering projects that have brought people closer together.

ØRESUND CROSSING

This bridge-and-tunnel crossing is the first land link between Sweden and the rest of Europe. It makes traveling quicker, so it is easier for Scandinavians to trade, socialize, and connect with each other and the rest of Europe. It also includes a data cable for Internet transmission, so virtual communication is easier and more reliable. Building the crossing had unexpected benefits: the underwater parts have become an artificial reef, home to marine animals.

CHANNEL TUNNEL

This underwater tunnel links Great Britain with continental Europe. Creating a link had been an idea since the early 1800s, but it wasn't until 1988 that tunneling began. Eleven tunnel-boring machines worked from the English and French sides. They met in the middle in 1990, and passengers and goods were able to travel on trains through the tunnel from 1994. Rail travel is now possible from Great Britain to all of Europe.

SATELLITES

The first communication satellites were launched in the 1960s. Today much of our everyday lives depend on satellites beaming information around the world, from long-distance communication by phone and the Internet to live television broadcasts and finding our way by GPS. Satellites also help track weather and other natural phenomena. Signals are beamed up to satellites orbiting Earth and then beamed back to a different place—traveling far quicker than they could by land.

TRANS-SIBERIAN RAILROAD

The idea behind the Trans-Siberian Railroad was to encourage Russians to move east to Siberia and to help Russia trade with east Asia. Building began in 1891. Huge numbers of people worked to build the route through thick forests, rocky mountains, and soggy bogs. Even today a lot of maintenance is needed to keep the railroad level—the ground shifts when winter permafrost thaws, which makes the tracks buckle.

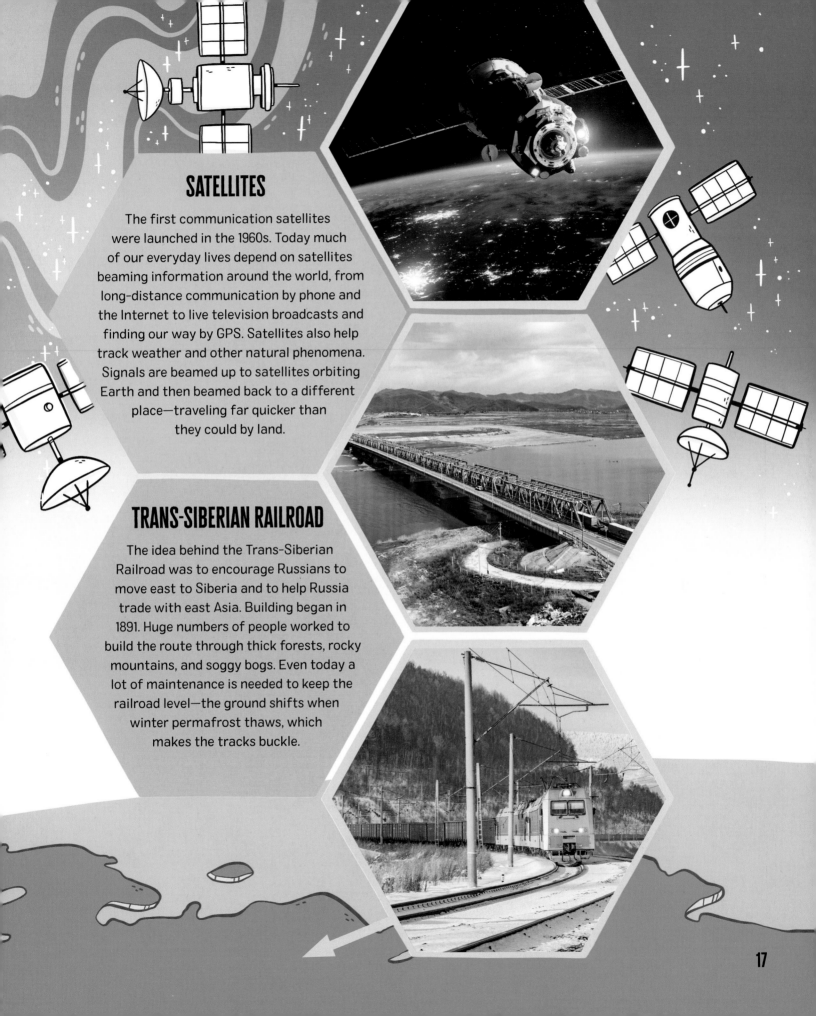

TRANSPORTATION

Engineering keeps us moving! Civil engineers help build the roads, bridges, tunnels, and railroads that connect us. Mechanical engineers help create the vehicles that we travel in. Engineers are always looking to build better ways to travel well in a changing world.

TRAINS

Steam engines were first developed to move heavy goods such as coal and slate from mines so that horses no longer had to do the work. At first, passengers were worried about the dangers of traveling fast, but within years railroads had changed lives for millions of people in Victorian Britain.

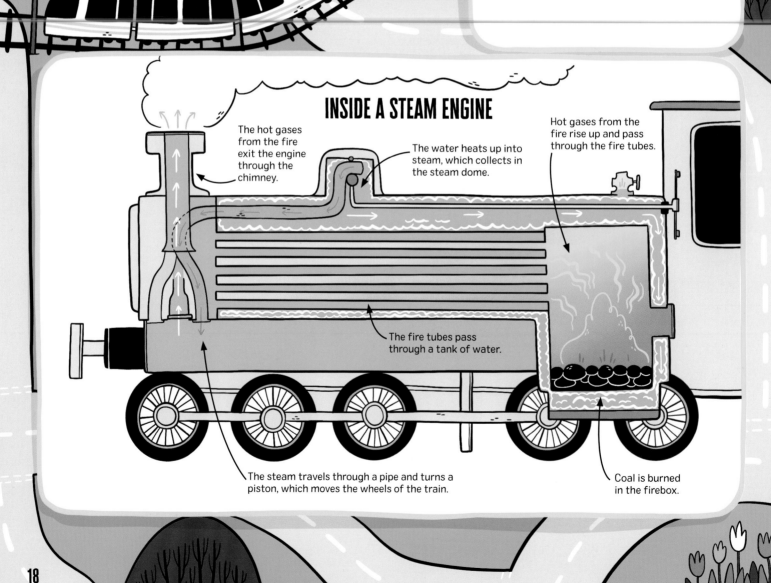

INSIDE A STEAM ENGINE

The hot gases from the fire exit the engine through the chimney.

The water heats up into steam, which collects in the steam dome.

Hot gases from the fire rise up and pass through the fire tubes.

The fire tubes pass through a tank of water.

The steam travels through a pipe and turns a piston, which moves the wheels of the train.

Coal is burned in the firebox.

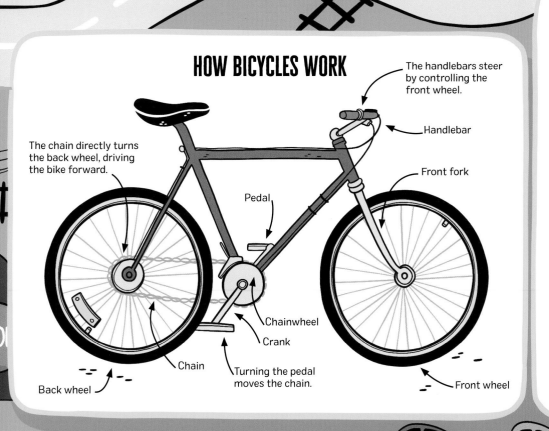

HOW BICYCLES WORK

The handlebars steer by controlling the front wheel.

Handlebar

Front fork

The chain directly turns the back wheel, driving the bike forward.

Pedal

Chainwheel

Crank

Chain

Turning the pedal moves the chain.

Back wheel

Front wheel

BICYCLES

The first modern bicycle was made in 1888. Since then, engineers have made many changes to improve bicycle designs. Different sizes and thicknesses of wheels work for different speeds and surfaces. Different gears make it easier to cycle uphill or give more power on flat terrain.

This century, there have two major new developments in bicycle design. **Folding bikes** can be easily carried on trains and used to finish trips, while **electric bikes** can help people travel longer distances on their bikes.

CARS

The motorized car was invented in 1886 by Karl Benz. Motor engines use energy from the combustion (burning) of fuel to power the piston. This is efficient, and most cars are still powered in this way, but these engines use unsustainable, polluting fossil fuels.

Electric cars are a more environmentally friendly way of driving. Their rechargable batteries store chemical energy that powers the car's electric motor.

In combustion engines, the more the foot presses on the accelerator (gas pedal), the more fuel reaches the engine, which gives it more power and speeds up the car. In an electric car, the more the accelerator is pressed, the greater the voltage that is sent from the battery to the motor.

HOW ELECTRIC CAR ENGINES WORK

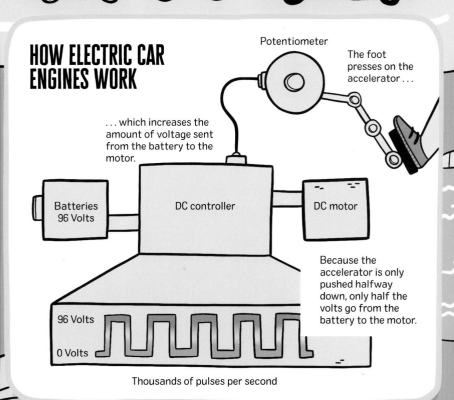

Potentiometer

The foot presses on the accelerator . . .

. . . which increases the amount of voltage sent from the battery to the motor.

Batteries 96 Volts

DC controller

DC motor

Because the accelerator is only pushed halfway down, only half the volts go from the battery to the motor.

96 Volts

0 Volts

Thousands of pulses per second

PROTECTION FROM NATURAL DISASTERS

The best engineering works with nature in mind. Nature can be powerful in strong and surprising ways. Some forces, such as earthquakes, storms, and floods, can damage and destroy buildings. Engineers find ways to keep us safe inside structures, even in the face of the world's most powerful forces.

Tokyo's tallest building is built with the same engineering as a pagoda, to protect it from earthquakes.

Tokyo Skytree

Traditional Japanese pagoda

EARTHQUAKE-PROOF BUILDINGS

When an earthquake strikes, the biggest danger is from being trapped or injured by a collapsed building. For centuries, Japanese buildings have been made with the knowledge they could be destroyed by an earthquake. Traditional buildings are designed to collapse in the least dangerous way: walls are light—built from paper and wood rather than heavy stone—and can be rebuilt easily. Modern buildings in danger zones can be engineered to shake with an earthquake without being damaged or destroyed. They are built with a strong central column with balancing struts that help steady them.

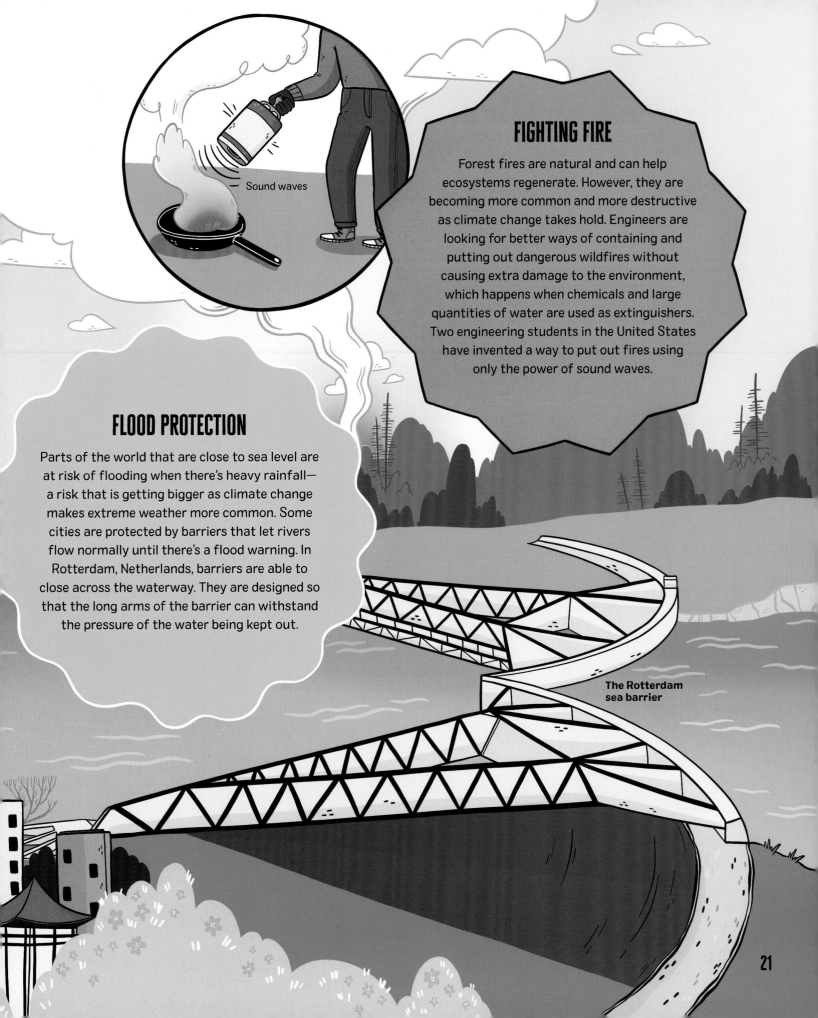

FIGHTING FIRE

Forest fires are natural and can help ecosystems regenerate. However, they are becoming more common and more destructive as climate change takes hold. Engineers are looking for better ways of containing and putting out dangerous wildfires without causing extra damage to the environment, which happens when chemicals and large quantities of water are used as extinguishers. Two engineering students in the United States have invented a way to put out fires using only the power of sound waves.

Sound waves

FLOOD PROTECTION

Parts of the world that are close to sea level are at risk of flooding when there's heavy rainfall—a risk that is getting bigger as climate change makes extreme weather more common. Some cities are protected by barriers that let rivers flow normally until there's a flood warning. In Rotterdam, Netherlands, barriers are able to close across the waterway. They are designed so that the long arms of the barrier can withstand the pressure of the water being kept out.

The Rotterdam sea barrier

WATER

Water is vital for life: we need it to drink and to cook, wash, and keep clean with. When we turn on a faucet, it's engineers we can thank for bringing fresh, clean water to our homes. In places where there is no plumbing, where there's no safe water supply, or where dirty water is left standing and parasites can grow, the finding and fetching of clean, safe water can take up a large part of a person's day—time when they could be going to school, studying, or earning money. Here's how engineering keeps water flowing through your daily life.

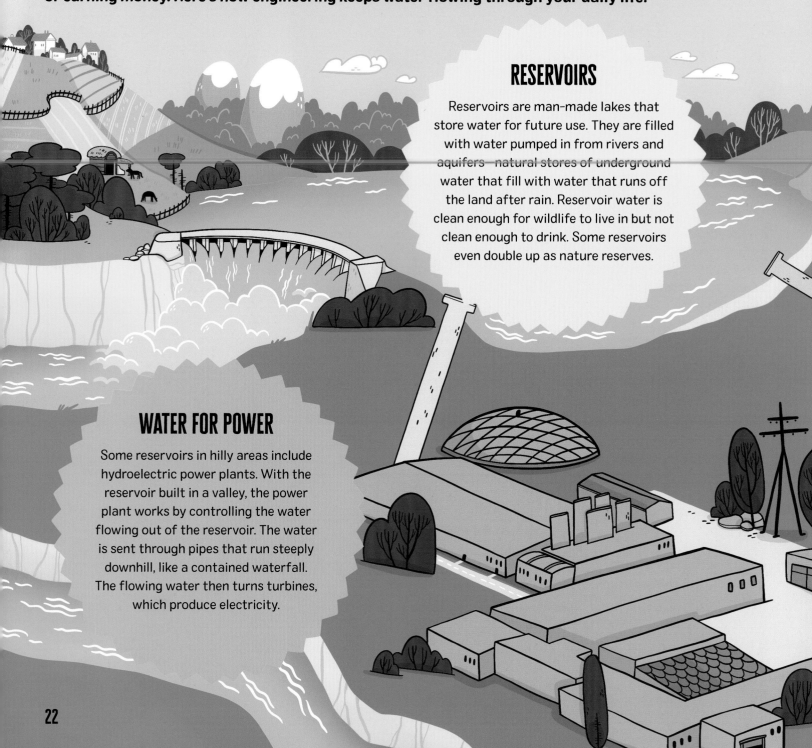

RESERVOIRS

Reservoirs are man-made lakes that store water for future use. They are filled with water pumped in from rivers and aquifers—natural stores of underground water that fill with water that runs off the land after rain. Reservoir water is clean enough for wildlife to live in but not clean enough to drink. Some reservoirs even double up as nature reserves.

WATER FOR POWER

Some reservoirs in hilly areas include hydroelectric power plants. With the reservoir built in a valley, the power plant works by controlling the water flowing out of the reservoir. The water is sent through pipes that run steeply downhill, like a contained waterfall. The flowing water then turns turbines, which produce electricity.

REYHAN JAMALOVA (BORN 2002)

Growing up in a small village in rural Azerbaijan with an unreliable electricity supply, Reyhan Jamalova knew very well that when heavy rain causes power blackouts, people's lives are put on hold. When she was just fourteen years old, she came up with an idea: to harvest the energy of heavy rain and use it to produce electricity. Jamalova founded the company Rainergy, aiming to bring electricity to less developed places and to make the best of the heavy rain. Her device collects rainwater, which then flows through a generator at high speed, producing electricity. The electricity can be stored in a battery, ready for use exactly when it's needed.

WASTEWATER

Dirty water is taken away from your home when you flush the toilet or empty the sink. More detail is given on pages 36 and 37.

WATER FOR DRINKING

Water treatment plants take water from reservoirs and rivers and make it safe for drinking. The water is treated with chemicals to remove some of the dirt and particles in it—they clump together and sink to the bottom of the tank. The clear water left at the top passes through many filters to remove tiny particles such as dust, bacteria, and microbes. Finally, the water is disinfected with chemicals such as chlorine. It is then safe to drink and can be piped out to people's homes.

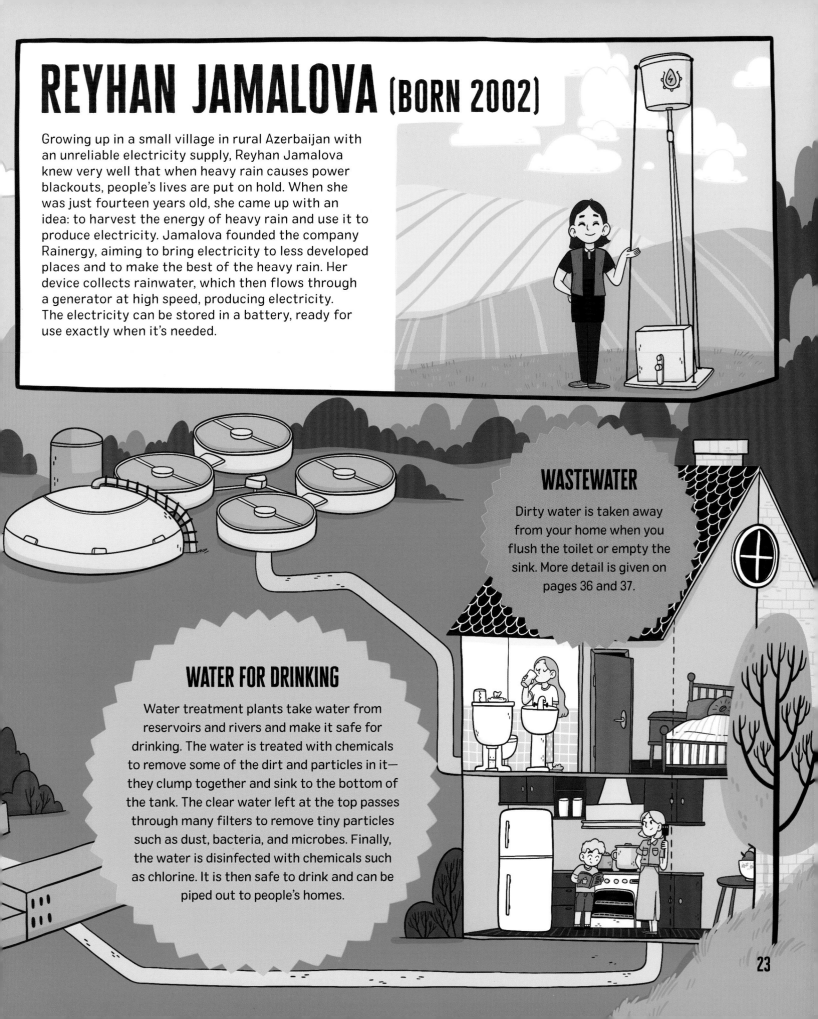

THE POWER GRID

POWER PLANTS

Most countries run their power grid from a mix of sources. These are the types of power plants that are available to them:

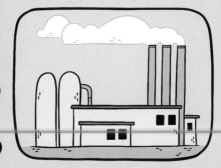

Natural gas

Around one-fourth of the world's electricity comes from burning natural gas to power turbines. Natural gas is a fossil fuel that was created underground over millions of years, and one day it will run out. Power plants fired by natural gas produce greenhouse gases, which contribute to climate change.

A power grid is a way of sending electricity across a country so that everyone has access to electricity, even if they live far away from a power plant. It is a network of cables that carries high-voltage electricity from power plants (where the electricity is made) to substations, where its power (the voltage) is reduced so that electricity can be safely sent to homes and other buildings nearby. When you plug in your devices or switch on lights and other appliances, the electricity you use comes from your local substation. Connecting many power plants together means that the production of electricity can be shared across a vast area.

DID YOU KNOW?

The first national power grid system was created in Britain in the 1930s.

Coal

This fossil fuel is burned at coal power plants to create electricity. It was first used to produce electricity in the 1880s. Coal is cheap, but it produces a lot of greenhouse gases, so many countries are trying to switch to greener electricity sources.

Nuclear power plants

These power plants generate heat to turn turbines, by splitting atoms of uranium. Nuclear power is more efficient than burning fossil fuels, and it doesn't produce any greenhouse gases. However, the waste products from this process are radioactive, dangerous, and hard to dispose of.

Wind turbines

These turbines produce electricity when the wind spins their sails around. The stronger the wind, the more electricity the turbine can produce. Wind turbines are built in exposed, windy places. They can't produce power when there's no wind.

Biomass

Power plants can burn biomass—plant and animal material such as wood pellets or farm waste. The heat created is used to power turbines and create electricity. Biomass is renewable, but burning it does create greenhouse gases.

Hydropower

Hydroelectric power plants use falling water to turn turbines, generating electricity.

Solar

Solar panels use energy from the Sun to produce electricity. They are particularly useful in places where the sun shines all year round. The stronger the Sun shines, the more electricity solar panels can produce. Solar panels can store energy in batteries, to be used later on.

FUTURE CARBON-FREE ELECTRICITY

To help protect against climate change, the world needs to generate most of its electricity in ways that do not produce greenhouse gases. This means no more burning coal or natural gas and increasing the amount of solar, wind, and hydro power we use. If more people can power their own homes and devices with electricity generated in an environmentally friendly way, we will become less reliant on power grids.

Here are some new technologies engineers are developing that might help people generate their own electricity in the future:

Solar-cell windows

These windows contain tiny, solar-energy-generating cells in the glass. So whenever light shines through them, it will make small amounts of electricity. The windows are still see-through even though they contain solar cells.

Breeze power

Mini wind turbines are being designed to sit on top of roofs and window ledges. They aim to capture even the very smallest breezes and create small electrical currents.

Backpack power up

This backpack is designed to capture the movement energy that is created as its wearer walks along. With each movement, a device in the backpack could create an electrical pulse, which could charge a small device such as a phone or an LED light.

Air or ground heat pump

This unit sits outside a house and can heat or cool the building without using much electricity. The pump uses heat from the air or ground to warm a fluid that then heats or cools the inside of the home, in a way similar to how refrigerators work.

EXPLORATION

Throughout history, engineering has enabled people to explore the world. With newly invented tools and machines, we have been able to move from places that feel safe into unexplored, unknown, and potentially dangerous places. People have explored and settled in more places, met more people, and learned ever more about the world. We have also been inspired to engineer even more amazing machines!

COMPASS

The compass was invented more than 2,000 years ago in China. People noticed that some rocks naturally attract and repel each other—these are natural magnets called lodestones. People then realized that Earth is like one enormous magnet, and that a magnet will always want to point north. So engineers started designing ways to allow a magnet the freedom to move by itself—in a compass. That way, wherever you were, the compass could always show you which way was north.

UNDERWATER EXPLORATION

Even today, we have only explored around 5% of the world's oceans! Deep underwater it is cold and dark, with very high pressure. The salt water corrodes equipment and conducts electricity, so technology designed for exploring the deep sea has to resist all of these things, as well as provide oxygen for the explorer to breathe. Here are some ways we have helped ourselves look deeper than the shoreline.

Cord for lowering the craft into the sea.

Three thick windows made of fused quartz —the strongest transparent material available at the time.

Spherical shape, for resisting the strong pressure of being deep underwater

THE BATHYSPHERE (1930-1934)

U.S. engineer Otis Barton designed this spherical diving device so that naturalist William Beebe could explore the deep sea and observe the animals in their environment. It allowed humans to travel farther underwater than ever before, reaching depths of 3,028 ft. (923 m) below sea level.

UNDERWATER REMOTELY OPERATED VEHICLE (ROV)

ROVs are robots that are attached to a ship by cables so the ROV and operator can communicate. The robots use video cameras, lights, and robotic arms to collect samples. The researchers on the boat control the ROV's movements and analyze the information it sends back.

AUTONYMOUS UNDERWATER VEHICLE (AUV)

AUVs work underwater without a human nearby, but they are not tethered to the ship. The work they do is programmed into them by a controller before the AUV enters the water.

SPACE EXPLORATION

Space is a vacuum, which means there is no air pressure. If we were to enter space in our normal clothes, we would quickly pass out and die, because our bodies need pressure around us to function properly. So spacecraft and space suits need to be artificially pressurized. There's also very little gravity in space, which means a lot of small but important engineering decisions need to be made when designing spacecraft in order to enable astronauts to do their daily jobs. Here are some of the features of our largest spacecraft, the International Space Station.

Foot- and handholds on the outside of the spacecraft help astronauts anchor themselves when they are out on space walks.

Drinking water is kept in vacuum bags with a straw. In a glass it would float around and not stay in the cup.

Astronauts have to do daily exercise, such as running and weight lifting, because their bones and muscles weaken without gravity.

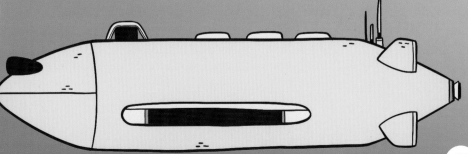

PROTECTING THE ENVIRONMENT

Our modern lives affect the natural world. We cut down forests to build homes and to farm cattle, and we use pesticides to kill off creatures that could eat or harm our crops and plants. Our cars, factories, and homes give off polluting gases that warm the planet and make it hard to breathe. Engineering has created many of these problems, but engineering is also one of the best ways we have of finding ways to help the environment and solve the climate crisis.

CAPTURING CARBON

It will be some time before we can stop putting so much carbon dioxide into the air. One way of stopping carbon dioxide levels from getting too high is to remove it from the air. Some power plants will capture carbon dioxide before it even leaves the building. In other places, such as Iceland and Switzerland, large machines remove the gas from the air and put it somewhere safe, such as underground, where it will eventually turn into rock.

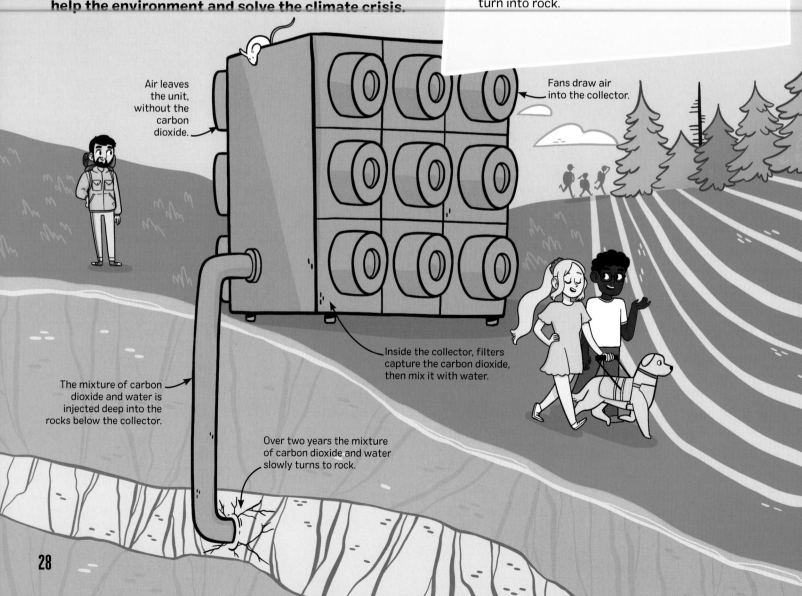

Air leaves the unit, without the carbon dioxide.

Fans draw air into the collector.

Inside the collector, filters capture the carbon dioxide, then mix it with water.

The mixture of carbon dioxide and water is injected deep into the rocks below the collector.

Over two years the mixture of carbon dioxide and water slowly turns to rock.

ROBOT TREE PLANTERS

Trees take in carbon dioxide and release oxygen, so planting them helps fight climate change. Two new robot tree planters have been invented to plant thousands of trees as quickly as possible. The first robot carries up to 300 tree seedlings at a time and can plant between 1,000 and 3,500 trees in six hours. The second robot is a brush cutter, which carefully cuts away any other vegetation growing around each seedling in order to give the trees the best chance of growing successfully. The inventors of these robots hope that they will eventually be able to plant trees and make decisions without any human supervision.

CARBON COMPETITION

The Carbon XPrize is a competition that encourages inventors to turn carbon dioxide into useful products. Here are a few of the amazing products that have been made out of thin air so far.

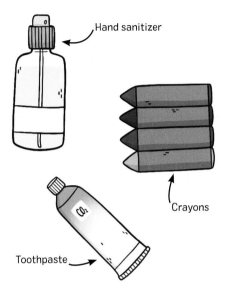

Hand sanitizer

Crayons

Toothpaste

COASTLINES

With rising sea levels, more parts of the world need help to protect their coastlines. There are two ways to do this. **Hard engineering** uses man-made structures such as sea walls to protect the land. These stop powerful waves from washing away land, sand, rocks, and plants. However, they are expensive to build and keep up, and they can destroy natural ecosystems. **Soft engineering** works with nature to help protect land, and it tends to be less expensive. Adding natural plants around beaches and coasts helps soften the power of the sea and stabilizes the land so that it is less likely to be washed away.

HOW A SEA WALL WORKS

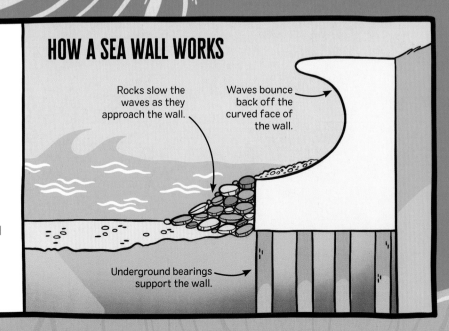

Rocks slow the waves as they approach the wall.

Waves bounce back off the curved face of the wall.

Underground bearings support the wall.

FUTURE-PROOFING

Our world is changing. Our weather systems are less predictable than they used to be, so we can't know for sure what the next few decades will be like—but we do know we are likely to have more extreme weather, with hotter summers and more rain. Our towns and cities need clever civil engineering to help us live with the new climates and the challenges they will bring. This imaginary city features some of the ways engineers already work with the changing weather, as well as some things that might come into use in the future.

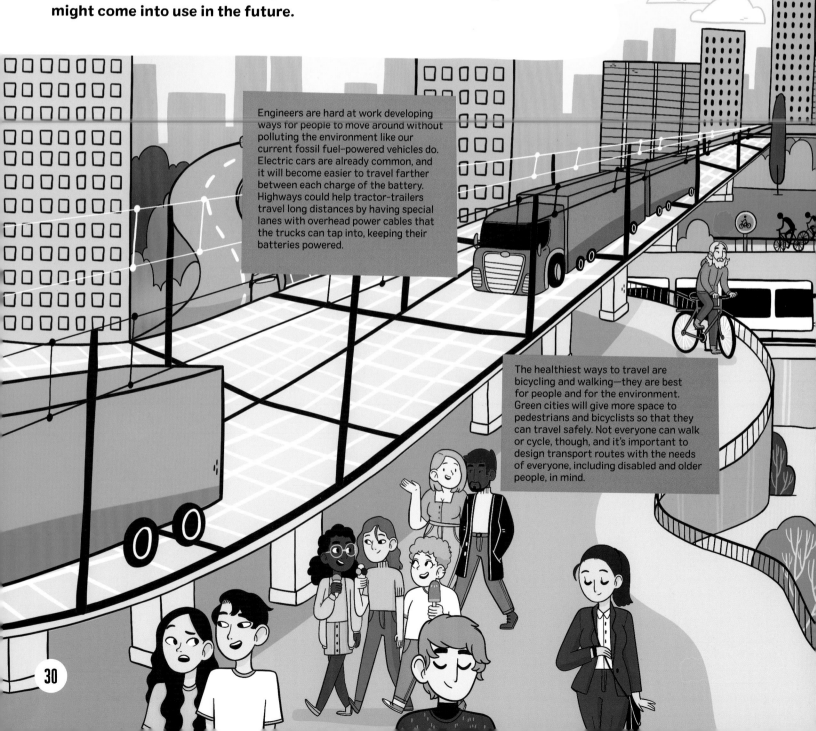

Engineers are hard at work developing ways for people to move around without polluting the environment like our current fossil fuel–powered vehicles do. Electric cars are already common, and it will become easier to travel farther between each charge of the battery. Highways could help tractor-trailers travel long distances by having special lanes with overhead power cables that the trucks can tap into, keeping their batteries powered.

The healthiest ways to travel are bicycling and walking—they are best for people and for the environment. Green cities will give more space to pedestrians and bicyclists so that they can travel safely. Not everyone can walk or cycle, though, and it's important to design transport routes with the needs of everyone, including disabled and older people, in mind.

As the climate is gets warmer we will want to keep our homes and buildings cool, but ideally without using lots of electricity. Buildings can be designed to make use of shade and natural air ventilation. Smart shutters on windows can sense light and heat and close automatically, to stop the inside getting too warm, with big awnings providing shade.

ROTTERDAM

Rotterdam, Netherlands, has always lived with water. It's a port town on the coast, where three big rivers empty into the North Sea, and its land is close to sea level. As the settlement grew, it needed to protect itself from the sea, and its first dams were built in the 1100s. Now Rotterdam leads the world in engineering for living with rain and water.

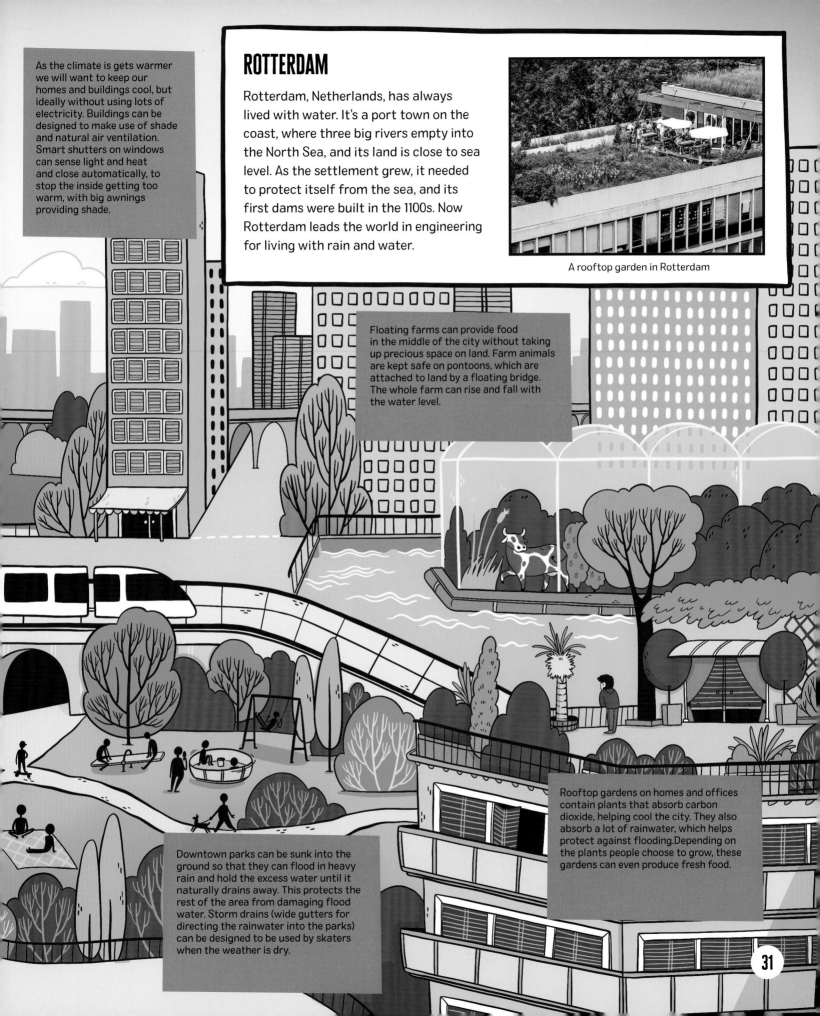

A rooftop garden in Rotterdam

Floating farms can provide food in the middle of the city without taking up precious space on land. Farm animals are kept safe on pontoons, which are attached to land by a floating bridge. The whole farm can rise and fall with the water level.

Rooftop gardens on homes and offices contain plants that absorb carbon dioxide, helping cool the city. They also absorb a lot of rainwater, which helps protect against flooding. Depending on the plants people choose to grow, these gardens can even produce fresh food.

Downtown parks can be sunk into the ground so that they can flood in heavy rain and hold the excess water until it naturally drains away. This protects the rest of the area from damaging flood water. Storm drains (wide gutters for directing the rainwater into the parks) can be designed to be used by skaters when the weather is dry.

WHEELCHAIRS

The wheelchair is a wonderful piece of mechanical engineering that has been helping people move around since at least the times of ancient Greece and China. This invention has been improved on over the centuries, allowing more people to join in with the social, economic, and cultural life of their communities.

TIME LINE

It's hard to know for sure when the first wheelchair was made, but we know one was used by King Philip of Spain (1527–1598), who had gout. Gout can make walking painful, so Philip was pushed around by a servant. Here are a few of the developments in wheelchair technology that followed.

1655 German clockmaker Stephan Farfler invented the first self-propelled wheelchair. He had broken his back as a child and couldn't use his legs. As a clockmaker he also had the skills needed to bring his invention to life. The chair had handles, cranks, and cogwheels that powered the front wheel.

1783 The Bath chair was designed to be steered by the sitter but pushed by someone else. Even Queen Victoria of Britain had one in her later years.

1958 The "Model 8" could be moved by someone pushing the handles or by the sitter pushing the wheels. It could be folded when not needed and is still used a lot in hospitals and nursing homes.

1990s When sports wheelchairs were developed, wheelchair users were given more than just a means of getting around—they could also join the world of competitive and leisure sports.

DAVID AGUILAR (BORN 1999)

David Aguilar is from Andorra. He always loved building and creating, and he spent his childhood making cars, planes, and motorcycles from toy bricks. Aguilar was born with an undeveloped right arm. It didn't hold him back, but he was annoyed by people always commenting on it.

When Aguilar was nine years old, he made himself his first prosthetic arm from toy bricks. It wasn't very strong, but it showed he could use the bricks to build something useful that he wanted.

He improved his design using technical building bricks. His new version, the MK1, took five days to build. He could use this new prosthetic arm to do push-ups!

Aguilar continued making upgrades to his invention. The MK2 can do much more. It can work like a bicep, using a combination of a battery and fishing cable. Aguilar can now move his arm up as far as he wants.

When Aguilar wore his homemade arm to school for the first time, everybody stared at it. Now he felt proud that people were talking about him and his arm.

ENGINEERING FOR THRILLS

Engineering is not always serious. Engineers like to create fun too, and to engineer things for people to enjoy! Civil engineers can turn ordinary structures into exhilarating experiences or use their knowledge of physics to create buildings and machines whose only function is our enjoyment.

LIANJIANG RIVER GLASS BRIDGE

More than sixty glass bridges have been built in China since 2016. They allow people to look directly down while crossing from one side of a dramatic ravine to the other. Whether you find this beautiful or terrifying depends on your fear of heights! The longest glass-bottomed bridge in the world crosses the Lianjiang River in Guangdong, China. It sits 660 ft. (201 m) above the river and is 1,726 ft. (526.14 m) long. The bridge can hold up to 500 people at a time.

ROLLER COASTERS

Civil engineers use simple physics to make a thrilling ride. Although the excitement is huge and the twists can be complicated, roller coasters are actually quite simple. The ride requires power only to bring the roller coaster up to the top of the first hill. The rest of the ride is powered solely by the kinetic and gravitational energy that builds up as the car climbs the first hill. Once it drops down the other side, gravity pulls the car down, and it gathers speed. Kinetic energy (the energy of movement) powers the car around the rest of the track.

HOVERBOARDS

These boards allow people to whiz along while staying balanced, owing to the mechanical engineering inside the board. The board is actually two boards—one for each wheel—that pivot around the center. Inside each wheel is an electric motor that makes it go, and sensors that detect tilt and speed. The information from the sensors helps keep the board upright. When the rider's feet are flat, the wheels are told to stay still. When the rider leans forward, the tilt sensor starts the wheels turning. Each wheel has its own sensors and motor so the wheels can move independently, allowing the hoverboard to spin in circles.

TOILETS

Some of the most important engineering in your life is also the smelliest. It took a series of deadly cholera epidemics in London, England, for the city to commission civil engineers to build a vast underground sewer system that is still in use today. Keeping sewage safely away from people has enabled us to live longer, with less disease. Sewers and water treatment are extremely important! Here's what happens to your waste after you you flush the toilet.

1. When you flush the toilet by pushing a lever or button, you open a valve in the cistern (tank of water), which lets the water empty into the toilet. The clean water rushes through holes in the toilet rim, washing the bowl clean while flushing its contents away.

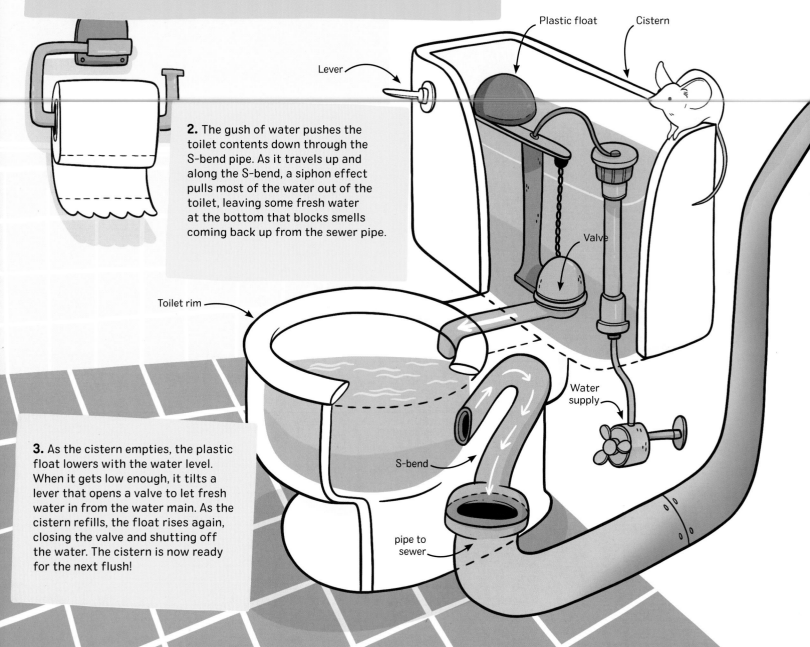

Plastic float

Cistern

Lever

2. The gush of water pushes the toilet contents down through the S-bend pipe. As it travels up and along the S-bend, a siphon effect pulls most of the water out of the toilet, leaving some fresh water at the bottom that blocks smells coming back up from the sewer pipe.

Valve

Toilet rim

Water supply

3. As the cistern empties, the plastic float lowers with the water level. When it gets low enough, it tilts a lever that opens a valve to let fresh water in from the water main. As the cistern refills, the float rises again, closing the valve and shutting off the water. The cistern is now ready for the next flush!

S-bend

pipe to sewer

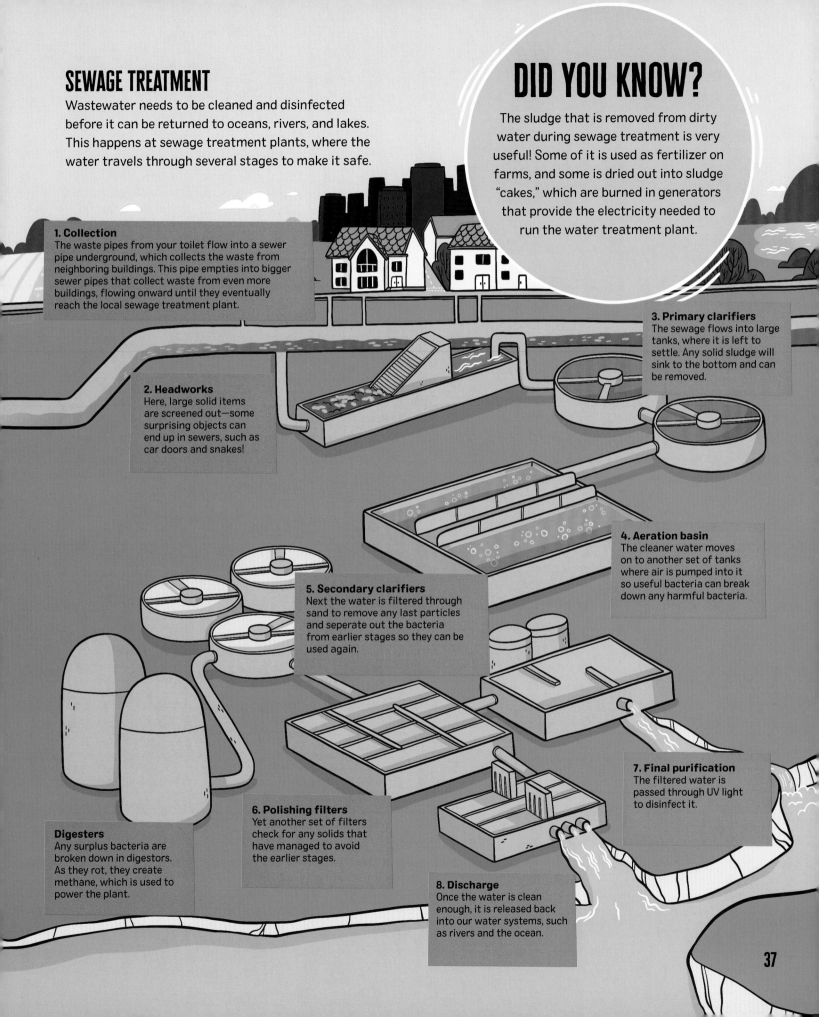

SEWAGE TREATMENT

Wastewater needs to be cleaned and disinfected before it can be returned to oceans, rivers, and lakes. This happens at sewage treatment plants, where the water travels through several stages to make it safe.

DID YOU KNOW?

The sludge that is removed from dirty water during sewage treatment is very useful! Some of it is used as fertilizer on farms, and some is dried out into sludge "cakes," which are burned in generators that provide the electricity needed to run the water treatment plant.

1. Collection
The waste pipes from your toilet flow into a sewer pipe underground, which collects the waste from neighboring buildings. This pipe empties into bigger sewer pipes that collect waste from even more buildings, flowing onward until they eventually reach the local sewage treatment plant.

2. Headworks
Here, large solid items are screened out—some surprising objects can end up in sewers, such as car doors and snakes!

3. Primary clarifiers
The sewage flows into large tanks, where it is left to settle. Any solid sludge will sink to the bottom and can be removed.

4. Aeration basin
The cleaner water moves on to another set of tanks where air is pumped into it so useful bacteria can break down any harmful bacteria.

5. Secondary clarifiers
Next the water is filtered through sand to remove any last particles and seperate out the bacteria from earlier stages so they can be used again.

6. Polishing filters
Yet another set of filters check for any solids that have managed to avoid the earlier stages.

7. Final purification
The filtered water is passed through UV light to disinfect it.

Digesters
Any surplus bacteria are broken down in digestors. As they rot, they create methane, which is used to power the plant.

8. Discharge
Once the water is clean enough, it is released back into our water systems, such as rivers and the ocean.

DIY ENGINEERING

While everyone can think like an engineer, it's not always possible to bring engineering projects to life in your own home. However, the invention of 3D printers has made this easier. These printers act somewhat like inkjet printers, but instead of using ink they build up 3D models layer by layer. They can allow us to make things more quickly, more simply, or in a more environmentally friendly way.

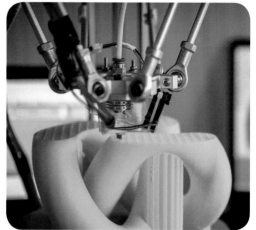

HOW 3D PRINTERS WORK

First, a 3D shape needs to be designed on a computer. The design contains all the information needed to tell the 3D printer how to build (or print) the object.

Inside the printer is a supply of powder or plastic, which the machinery melts so that it can be positioned where needed. A nozzle moves, "printing" or squeezing out tiny pieces of melted plastic into very precise locations. It builds up the object one layer at a time, waiting until each layer has dried before adding the next. The layers fuse onto each other using glue, or under the power of UV light.

FUTURE FOOD

Although 3D printers usually work with plastic, they can print anything that can be easily melted and then set at room temperature—including food! We can already print paste-like food, such as mashed potatoes or melted chocolate. In the future each kitchen could have its own 3D printer that could print out a meal. We could even print out a portion of seeds and mushrooms and things for them to grow on, then leave it on the windowsill to grow into a full meal!

SHELTERS

Large 3D printers could use mud and clay to "print" 3D shelters for people, especially in situations where shelters are needed quickly, such as after a natural disaster. They could even be used to build temporary eco-friendly shelters for large gatherings. Because the shelters are built from earth, they could easily be dug back into the ground, leaving no trace.

BRIDGES

Amsterdam, Netherlands, is home to the very first 3D printed steel bridge. Amsterdam has a lot of bridges because it has so many canals. The benefit of 3D printing the bridge is that it used less material, making it more efficient. The bridge was "printed" elsewhere then put into position across the canal. Future 3D printers could build bridges in place, reducing the need for transportation. Other bridges have already been 3D printed using concrete.

PROSTHETIC ARM

Medicine and surgery will also be able to make use of 3D printing. It already allows us to make prosthetics that precisely fit a person's needs. Making prosthetics with a 3D printer can be cheaper and quicker than the traditional way, which involves making a cast. This new method of printing also works well for children, who need good quality but cheap prostheses, because the prostheses need to be replaced regularly, whenever the children grow.

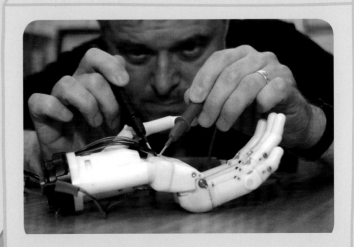

BUILDING WITH SPAGHETTI

This creative game will help you understand strength and structure, so you can think like a civil engineer.

YOUR TURN!

INSTRUCTIONS

1. Use the rigid spaghetti sticks as your structure's beams and columns, and the marshmallows as the cement to hold them together.

2. Decide on your structure—you could make a tower or a bridge or a simple shelter. You could even use a picture from this book as inspiration.

3. See how high or long you can build your structure. If it bends or breaks, what can you do to improve it?

4. Try adding more sticks of spaghetti to make a bundle, or snap them to make shorter lengths.

TAKE IT FURTHER

Try making this a competition with a friend. Set a timer for five minutes and see who can make the tallest tower or strongest bridge!

PROTOTYPE

A prototype is a model that engineers make out of easy materials before they scale their project up to life-size and use the final materials. Practice model making here by using cardboard, foil, and other materials to make a small model of a piece of furniture.

YOU WILL NEED
- A collection of items from your recycling, such as cardboard, foil, boxes, and cartons
- Play dough or clay
- Scissors
- Tape
- Glue
- Lollipop sticks

INSTRUCTIONS

1. Using the materials you have gathered, cut, shape, stick, and combine them to make a model of a chair. Depending on the size of the materials you have, your chair could be to support your weight or for a toy.

2. Try out your first attempt and fix anything that breaks or looks weak. How could you improve your prototype?

1

2

TAKE IT FURTHER

You could turn this into a game with a friend. Write down a few ideas for structures or problems to solve on slips of paper, then fold them up and put them in a bowl. Take turns picking one out and work together to make a model. Or make one each and see whose is the most successful.

RUBBER BAND CANNON

Ready to be a mechanical engineer? This explosive experiment shows you how different materials can combine and interact to make a blaster.

YOUR TURN!

WARNING:
Have an adult supervise!

YOU WILL NEED
- A large, empty potato chip tube
- An empty 20 fl. oz. (500 mL) water bottle that fits easily inside the tube
- Scissors
- Two rubber bands of the same size
- Clear tape or masking tape
- A pencil that is longer than the width of the tube
- Different balls or small toys to throw, or a ball made from scrunched-up aluminum foil

INSTRUCTIONS

1. Cut the end off the bottom of the tube so that it is open at both ends. Use the scissors carefully and ask an adult for help.

2. At one end of the tube, cut two slits about 1 in. (3 cm) deep, straight down from the top, about $\frac{1}{2}$ in. (1 cm) apart.

3. Repeat step 2 on the opposite side of the tube, so that you have two flaps facing each other. Don't wiggle the flaps—try to keep them stiff.

4. Loop one rubber band around each flap and gently pull down, so the length of the bands falls along the outside of the tube.

5. Use tape around the flaps to secure the bands in place and help strengthen the flaps.

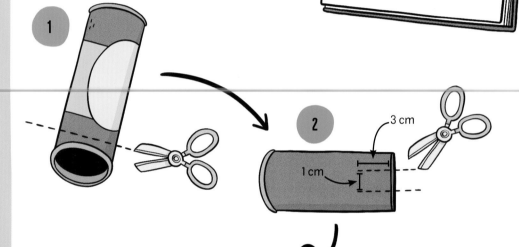

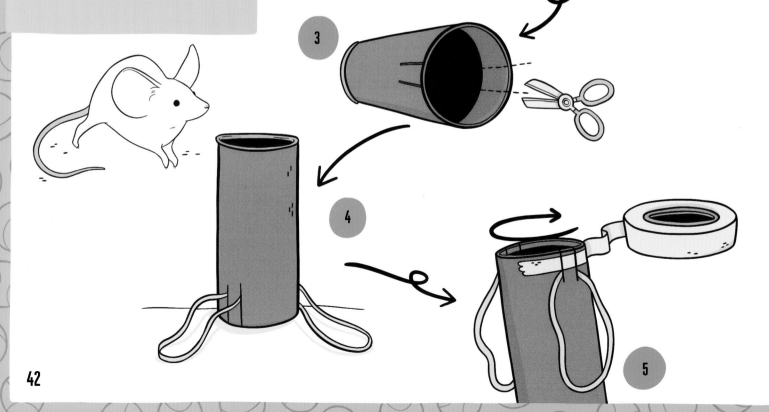

42

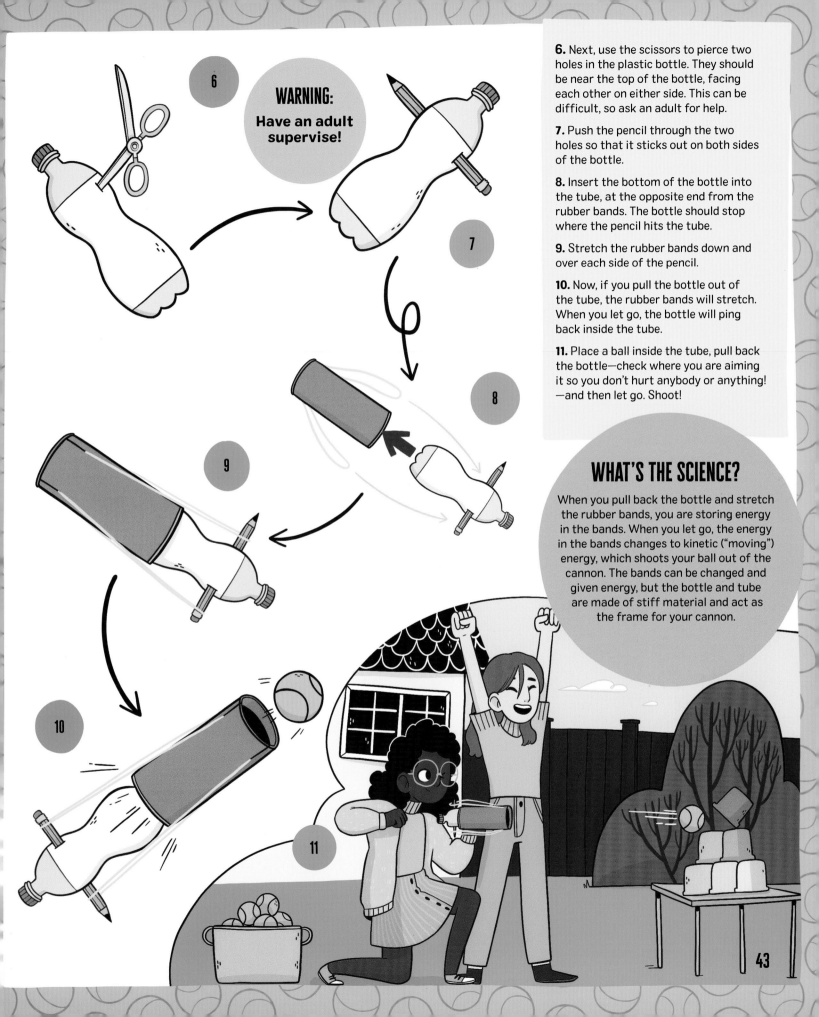

6. Next, use the scissors to pierce two holes in the plastic bottle. They should be near the top of the bottle, facing each other on either side. This can be difficult, so ask an adult for help.

7. Push the pencil through the two holes so that it sticks out on both sides of the bottle.

8. Insert the bottom of the bottle into the tube, at the opposite end from the rubber bands. The bottle should stop where the pencil hits the tube.

9. Stretch the rubber bands down and over each side of the pencil.

10. Now, if you pull the bottle out of the tube, the rubber bands will stretch. When you let go, the bottle will ping back inside the tube.

11. Place a ball inside the tube, pull back the bottle—check where you are aiming it so you don't hurt anybody or anything! —and then let go. Shoot!

WARNING:
Have an adult supervise!

WHAT'S THE SCIENCE?

When you pull back the bottle and stretch the rubber bands, you are storing energy in the bands. When you let go, the energy in the bands changes to kinetic ("moving") energy, which shoots your ball out of the cannon. The bands can be changed and given energy, but the bottle and tube are made of stiff material and act as the frame for your cannon.

BUILD A DOME

A dome is a 3D version of an arch, which is a very strong architectural device. We can see this is true because ancient buildings using arches are still standing today. Use strips of paper to build this dome and test its strength.

YOU WILL NEED

- A piece of card stock (stronger than normal paper but still able to bend)
- Scissors
- A split pin
- A rubber band
- A few flat objects of different weights, such as erasers and small toys

INSTRUCTIONS

1. Cut your card stock into several strips of the same size.

2. Line up the strips into a neat pile and find the center of the top strip.

3. Push a split pin through the center of the whole set of strips.

4. Fan out the strips as evenly as possible.

5. Use a rubber band to gather the ends and hold them in a dome structure. Don't make it too tight!

6. Now test out the dome's strength. How heavy an item can it hold up?

YOUR TURN!

WHAT'S THE SCIENCE?

Domes work by transferring the weight from the top of the dome to the bottom. The base of the dome (represented here by the rubber band) needs to be built thicker than the top in order to resist the forces and keep the dome together.

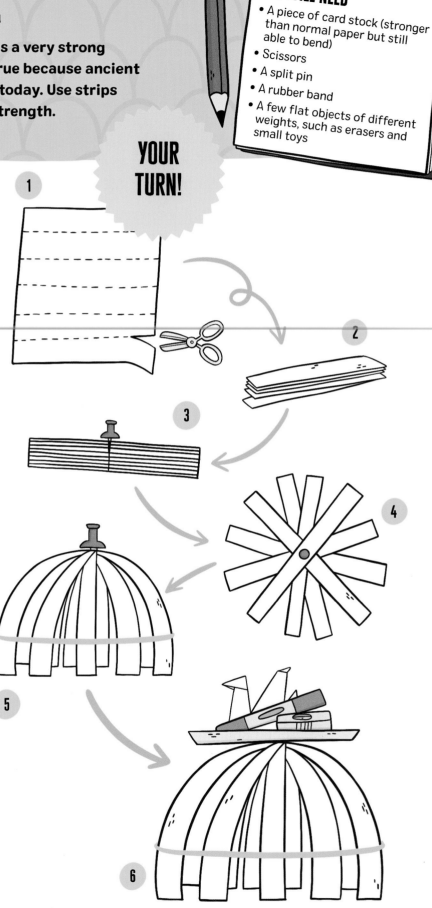

44

MAKE A WINDMILL

This activity explores simple turning mechanics. It also makes something beautiful!

YOU WILL NEED
- Squares of craft paper—you can use colored paper or decorate plain paper
- Scissors
- A small sticker
- Thin wooden dowel rod or stick
- Thumbtack

INSTRUCTIONS

1. Put two squares of paper on top of each other, neatly aligned. Using two different colors works well.

2. Fold the paper in half diagonally, then open it out again.

3. Repeat on the other diagonal.

4. Cut along each diagonal fold from the corner toward the center, but stop about 1 in. (2.5 cm) from the center.

5. Bend one corner from each flap in toward the center, but do not crease the fold. Secure the four corners in the middle using the sticker.

6. Secure the windmill onto its stick by pushing a thumbtack through the central sticker and onto the stick. The windmill needs to be able to spin, so don't press it in too tightly.

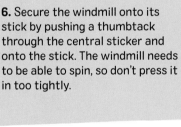

1

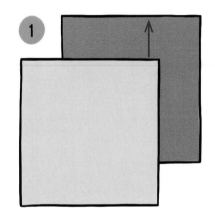

2

3

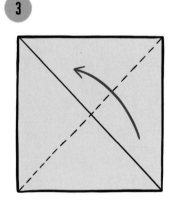

4

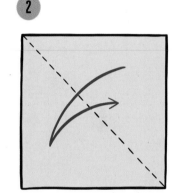

3 cm

5

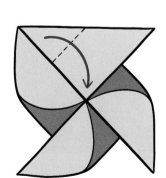

6

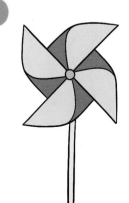

GLOSSARY

Aqueduct
A man-made structure for carrying water.

Commission
To order someone to do something, for example to pay them to do a piece of work such as building a railway or sewer.

Corrode
React with oxygen in air (or water) and break down or spoil. When iron corrodes, this is called rust.

Ecosystem
An environment and the community of living things interacting with it.

Epidemic
An outbreak of an infectious disease that affects many people in one place at the same time.

Fossil fuels
Fuels such as coal, oil and gas, which are burned to generate energy.

Foundation
The lowest part of a building, usually underground, that holds the building firm. Foundations can be shallow or deep.

Generator
A machine that makes electrical energy.

GPS
Global Positioning System—GPS devices use information sent by satellites around Earth to tell us exactly where we are.

Gravity
The force pulling objects toward each other or down to the ground.

Greenhouse gases
Gases that trap heat in the atmosphere and lead to global warming.

Microbes
Microscopic living things—e.g. bacteria.

Mortar
A paste used to glue bricks together in building. It is wet when used and dries rock hard.

Orbiting
Traveling around something, pulled by gravity. A planet orbits the stars and satellites orbit the Earth.

Parasite
A type of living thing that lives on or in another and causes it harm.

Patent
The right to use a particular invention. Inventors apply for patents so that they have the right to say the technology or idea of an invention belongs to them.

Permafrost
A thick layer of underground soil that stays frozen all year round.

Pesticides
Chemicals used to kill pests that might harm crops, such as insects or weeds.

Piston
A cylinder that moves back and forth inside a larger cylinder. In a car engine, the movement of the piston drives the rotating movement of the wheels.

Pontoon
A floating structure shaped like a flat-bottomed boat.

Radioactive
Giving off small particles of a certain type of energy that can be very dangerous.

Satellite
An object that revolves around a larger object in space. Moons are natural satellites. Artificial satellites include communications satellites, which orbit Earth.

Spire
A tall, pointed roof, especially of a church.

Suspension bridge
A kind of bridge in which the roadway hangs from strong cables, which in turn hang from towers.

Turbine
A machine that turns the movement of wind or moving water into energy.

Vacuum
Completely empty space.

Picture credits
The Publisher would like to thank the following for permission to reproduce their material.
Top = t; Bottom = b; Center = c; Left = l; Right = r

7 Drazen Zigic/Shutterstock; 12c kavram/Shutterstock, 12b Ivan Soto Cobos/Shutterstock; 13t fotohunter/Shutterstock, 13b Benson HE/Shutterstock; 16cl PA Images/Alamy Stock Photo, 16c qaphotos.com/Alamy Stock Photo, 16cr Bengt Hultqvist/Alamy Stock Photo; 17c RUSSAL/Shutterstock, 17T Dima Zel/Shutterstock, 17b Locomotive74/Shutterstock; 26 Soho A Studio/Shutterstock; 31t Frans Blok/Alamy Stock Photo; 32tl f8 archive/Alamy Stock Photo, 32tr Interfoto/Alamy Stock Photo, 32b Image Source/Alamy Stock Photo, 32bl Prill/Shutterstock; 38tl Wladimir Bulgar/Science Photo Library, 38c Xinhua/Alamy Stock Photo; 39t NASA/Science Photo Library, 39c Sipa US/Alamy Stock Photo, 39b Steve Linbridge/Alamy Stock Photo;

INDEX

THE AUTHOR & ILLUSTRATOR

JENNY JACOBY

Jenny writes and edits books and magazines for children. From writing science activity books to inspiring profiles, puzzles, and quizzes, she is passionate about making information fun. Jenny lives in London, England, with her family. Find out more at jennyjacoby.com.

LUNA VALENTINE

Luna Valentine is a Polish children's book illustrator living in Sheffield, England. She's inspired by science, nature, and witchcraft, and loves creating fun, lively characters who often get up to no good in their respective stories. When Luna's not drawing, it's only because one of her three pet rabbits has run off with her pencil.